CHALLEN

HOW
ARE Y

David Orme

CONTENTS

Introduction

'How fit are you?'

'Why is it important to be fit?'

If you don't want your car to break down you need to look after it!

To look after your car you should:

- give it the right sort of fuel
- make sure it has a service when it needs it
- keep it clean so it doesn't get rusty.

Your body is like a car. To keep it running properly, you should:

- give it the right sort of food
- have it checked out regularly
- look after it!

The best way to look after your body is to keep it busy with exercise.

This book will help you find out how fit you are, and show you why fitness matters!

QUIZ 1 Are you

Which do you choose?

Stairs? (1 point) A lift? (0 points)

For a short journey, do you:

Walk? (1 point) Ask for a ride in a car? (0 points)

At break time, do you:

Play outside? (1 point) Try to stay indoors? (0 points)

Do you do something active for at least half an hour every day?

Yes (1 point) No (0 points)

Do you do something very active, such as sport or dancing, at least three times a week?

Yes (1 point) No (0 points)

a couch potato?

Your score

5 points – Congratulations! You are a fitness champ!

4 points – Well done! You are serious about fitness.

3 points – Not bad … but room for improvement.

2 points – You're not doing enough to stay fit.

1 point – Get out of that chair and **do** something!

0 points – You are the couch potato champion – but **NO** medals!

QUIZ 2 Chips w

Do you eat fried food, such as chips, at least three times a week?

Yes (0 points) No (1 point)

Do you avoid eating vegetables?

Yes (0 points) No (1 point)

Do you drink mostly fizzy drinks?

Yes (0 points) No (1 point)

Do you eat things like crisps or biscuits most days?

Yes (0 points) No (1 point)

Would you rather have a chocolate bar than an apple?

Yes (0 points) No (1 point)

:h everything?

Your score

5 points – You are a healthy eating champ!

4 points – You are a fairly healthy eater.

3 points – Not bad … but could be better.

2 points – **Lots** of room for improvement.

1 point – You need to change your habits **NOW**.

0 points – You're a junk food fiend!

Why do we need to exercise?

Thousands of years ago, people had more exercise than now.

'Why?'

- They often had to hunt for their food.
- They might have had to run fast to escape from dangerous animals.
- They often walked long distances to find food.

These days, our bodies don't have to work so hard! Why?

- We don't have to walk – we can go by car.
- There aren't any dangerous animals waiting to chase us.
- Sometimes our food comes to us!

'Does this matter?'

Yes! Our bodies are designed to work hard. If they don't, things can start going wrong!

What can go wrong?

Exercise keeps our bodies working properly.

'What happens if we don't exercise?'

Lots of things!

- Important parts of our body, such as our heart, might stop working properly.
- **Arteries** and **veins** take blood round our bodies. Exercise keeps them healthy. If they do not work properly people can develop **high blood pressure**. This can lead to all sorts of illnesses.
- We might become overweight. This puts a strain on our heart. It can also lead to diseases such as **cancer** and **diabetes**.
- Exercise gives us strong bones. Weak bones can be a big problem when we are older.

Sometimes these problems only show up when we are older, but we need to try to prevent them now!

Moderate exercise

You should be moderately active for at least thirty minutes every day.

'What does *moderately* active mean?'

This is steady, regular exercise such as:

- walking
- cycling
- swimming
- working around the house.

You could:

- walk or cycle to school instead of going by car
- play a game at school break time – don't just sit around!
- play an outdoor game with friends
- help in the garden.

Even tidying your bedroom keeps you active!

Vigorous exercise

You should do vigorous exercise about three days a week, and for at least thirty minutes each time.

'What is *vigorous* exercise?'

This is exercise that makes your heart beat faster. It might make you sweat, or breathe faster, or feel tired.

You could:

- take part in a team game such as football
- do an athletic sport such as running
- join a club that teaches you the proper way to exercise.

'Does dancing count?'

Sure, if you move really fast!

Exercise is fun!

Joining a team or club will:

- help you to enjoy exercising
- make sure you exercise under safe conditions.

'What teams and clubs are there?'

There are lots to choose from! You could try ballet, gymnastics, yoga, football, aerobics and dozens of others.

'How can I find out about what is on offer where I live?'

One way is to ask at your local library.

'What about something a bit more unusual?'

You could take up one of the martial arts.

Martial arts is the name given to activities based on ancient fighting skills. Some people think they are violent, but anyone who takes part will tell you that this isn't true. The skills you learn should only be used in self-defence, never to hurt other people.

Anyone can soon learn the basic skills if they are prepared for a little hard work and a lot of practice.

The martial arts

'Which martial art could I take up?'

There are a lot to choose from.

One of the most ancient of the martial arts is kendo. This means "the way of the sword".

To practise kendo you need special equipment including a padded head guard and a bamboo sword.

Most people have heard of karate and judo. Karate is a fighting system which involves learning special punches and kicks. You also have to learn to block your opponent's moves.

To do well in judo you have to learn how to fall safely.

You fight in pairs and have to try to trip or throw your opponent. The winner is the one who keeps his or her opponent on the ground for a given time.

To do well in judo you have to learn how to fall safely.

Kung fu is very popular. It is based on Chinese martial arts. One form of kung fu led on to kick boxing.

Other forms of martial arts are aikido which teaches you how to beat your opponent without using much force, and tae kwon do which is like karate but with more types of kick.

Don't overdo it!

'What must I remember?'

It is important not to damage your body when it is still growing.

- Always warm up with gentle exercise before starting your vigorous exercise. This gets your **muscles** ready for action!
- Vigorous exercise is best every other day. This gives your body a day to recover.
- Don't try things that are meant for adults only, such as weightlifting.
- Always drink plenty of water when you are exercising.
- Don't forget any special clothes or equipment to keep you safe.
- It is best to stop your vigorous exercise gradually, not suddenly.

Gorgeous grub

No one can live without food – and we all love eating it!

'What does food do?'

- It gives us energy.
- It builds and repairs our bodies.
- It gives us the special chemicals that help our body to work properly.

'What is the best sort of food to eat?'

It is best to eat a wide range of food. We need to learn what isn't good for us if we eat too much of it.

'What is the best thing to drink?'

The best thing is water!

Fizzy drinks taste good, but can be full of sugar which can harm our teeth. People should drink about five glasses of water a day.

Energy food

'I want to eat well so I am fit, but I don't want to get fat.'

You need to think about what you eat.

Our energy comes from food that contains **fat**, **sugar** and **carbohydrates**.

Fat can come from meat, spreads and oil.

Sugar can come from sweets and chocolate.

Carbohydrates come from cereals, bread, potatoes and pasta.

Carbohydrates are the best way to get long-lasting energy. We should eat some every day.

If we eat more energy food than we need, especially sugar and fat, the body stores it up – and we get fat!

Ready-made food, such as biscuits, may contain lots of fat and sugar.

You can still enjoy good food without getting fat!

Look at the information on the package to find out what is in the food or drink.

NUTRITION	
Dry Pasta	
A 100g serving of pasta weighs approx, 320g when cooked	
TYPICAL COMPOSITION	A 100g (3 1/2 oz) serving provides
Energy	1463kj/345kcal
Protein	13.2g
Carbohydrate	68.5g
of which sugars	2.0g
Fat 2.0g	
of which saturates	0.4g
Fibre	2.9g
Sodium	trace
This pack contains 5 servings	
INFORMATION	

Food that builds and repairs

'What else should I eat as well as carbohydrates?'

The food that builds and repairs our bodies is called **protein**.

Protein comes from meat and fish. People who do not eat meat can eat eggs, cheese, nuts and beans as these are good protein foods.

'Are these foods always good for us?'

Yes, but it is best not to eat red meat more than three times a week as it is high in fat. Eat chicken and fish, or a **vegetarian** choice instead.

Try to eat two to three servings of these foods each day.

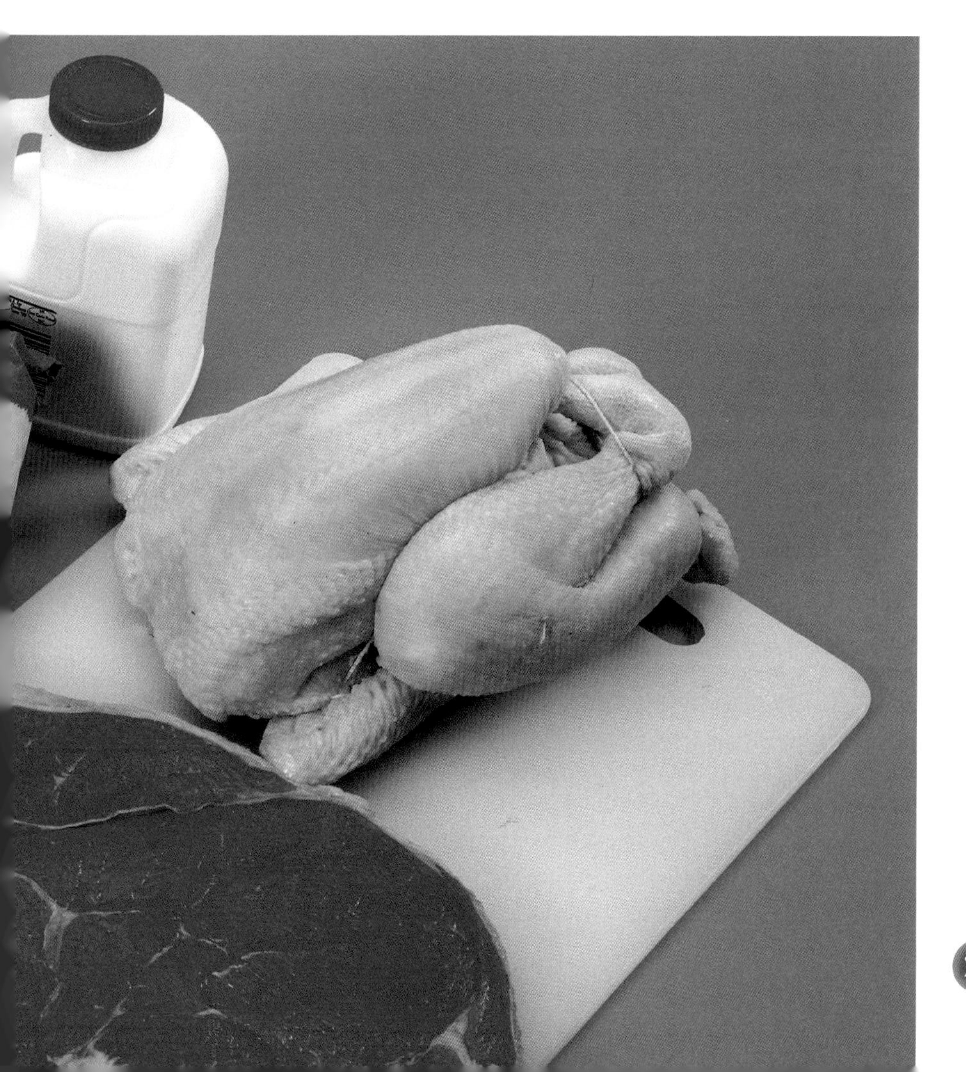

Food for keeping us well

The body needs other types of food if it is to work properly.

Chemicals called **vitamins** and **minerals** do special jobs in the body.

Calcium is a mineral. It is found in milk, butter and cheese. It builds strong teeth and bones.

Vitamin C is found in fruit and vegetables. It is important for keeping people healthy.

'Is there anything else we should eat?'

Fibre is another important part of our food.

Fibre helps us digest food properly.

Eating plenty of fruit and vegetables is a good way to make sure we have enough vitamins, minerals and fibre.

We should eat at least five servings of these every day.

Health dangers

Some things are very definitely bad for us!

'What sort of things?'

- smoking
- taking drugs
- drinking too much alcohol.

It causes serious diseases of the lungs, such as cancer. Around one in five smokers die early because they smoke.

No! Drugs such as **antibiotics** can help us when we are ill. But dangerous drugs, such as heroin and cocaine, have very serious effects on the body.

Too much alcohol damages the body and can cause accidents.

Because they are addicted – this means they can't stop.

Glossary

antibiotics medicines that can cure illnesses caused by germs or bacteria

arteries blood vessels that carry blood away from the heart

fat, sugar, carbohydrates the parts of food that give us energy

fibre the part of food that doesn't give us energy or build muscles but helps us digest what we have eaten

high blood pressure, cancer, diabetes serious illnesses sometimes caused by poor diet

muscles the parts of the body that shrink and stretch so that you can move

protein the part of a food that builds and repairs our body

vegetarian someone who does not eat meat

veins blood vessels that carry blood towards the heart

vitamins and minerals important chemicals in our food. We need these in very small amounts